D0998793

MY FIRST SPORTS

Skateboarding

by Ray McClellan

Note to Librarians, Teachers, and Parents:

Blastoff! Readers are carefully developed by literacy experts and combine standards-based content with developmentally appropriate text.

Level 1 provides the most support through repetition of high-frequency words, light text, predictable sentence patterns, and strong visual support.

Level 2 offers early readers a bit more challenge through varied simple sentences, increased text load, and less repetition of high-frequency words.

Level 3 advances early-fluent readers toward fluency through increased text and concept load, less reliance on visuals, longer sentences, and more literary language.

Level 4 builds reading stamina by providing more text per page, increased use of punctuation, greater variation in sentence patterns, and increasingly challenging vocabulary.

Level 5 encourages children to move from "learning to read" to "reading to learn" by providing even more text, varied writing styles, and less familiar topics.

Whichever book is right for your reader, Blastoff! Readers are the perfect books to build confidence and encourage a love of reading that will last a lifetime!

This edition first published in 2011 by Bellwether Media, Inc.

No part of this publication may be reproduced in whole or in part without written permission of the publisher. For information regarding permission, write to Bellwether Media, Inc., Attention: Permissions Department, 5357 Penn Avenue South, Minneapolis, MN 55419.

Library of Congress Cataloging-in-Publication Data
McClellan, Ray.
 Skateboarding / by Ray McClellan.
   p. cm. — (Blastoff! readers: My first sports)
 Includes bibliographical references and index.
 Summary: "Simple text and full-color photography introduce beginning readers to the sport of skateboarding. Developed by literacy experts for students in grades two through five"—Provided by publisher.
 ISBN 978-1-60014-462-2 (hardcover : alk. paper)
 1. Skateboarding—Juvenile literature. I. Title.
 GV859.8.M397 2010
 796.22—dc22   2010000792

Text copyright © 2011 by Bellwether Media, Inc. BLASTOFF! READERS and associated logos are trademarks and/or registered trademarks of Bellwether Media, Inc.

Printed in the United States of America, North Mankato, MN.
080110   1162

Contents

What Is Skateboarding?

Skateboarding is a sport where people ride and do tricks on skateboards. Skateboarding started in the 1950s. Surfers in California wanted something to do when they could not surf. They put roller skate wheels on the bottoms of flat boards. These were the first skateboards.

fun fact

Almost 200,000 people attended the 1995 Summer X Games.

Skateboarding has changed a lot since the 1950s. Skateboarders began doing tricks. By the 1980s, they were doing huge jumps off **ramps**.

The top skaters became **professionals**. The sport reached even more people with the start of the **Summer X Games** in 1995.

The Basic Rules of Skateboarding

There are many types of skateboarding competitions. The two most popular types are **street** and **vert**. Street skaters do a series of tricks on a street course. A street course has rails, jumps, and other obstacles. Judges score each skater on his or her routine. The skater with the highest score wins.

fun fact

In the Big Air event, skaters drop down a huge ramp and do tricks as they sail through the air. Jumps can be as long as 75 feet (23 meters)!

Vert skating is a high-flying sport. Skateboarders ride up and down a tall ramp. The most common ramp is a **half-pipe**.

They do flips, spins, **grabs**, and other tricks as they fly through the air. Judges score them on their tricks and the height of their jumps.

slalom

Many skateboarders also race. In downhill races, skateboarders speed down hills and around curves. They try to reach the finish line as fast as possible. **Slalom** courses have marked gates that riders must pass through.

Skateboarding Equipment

deck

trucks

fun fact

The angled end of a skateboard deck is called a kicktail. A rider can step down on the kicktail to launch the front of the board into the air.

The skateboard is the main piece of skateboarding gear. A skateboard has three main parts. They are the **deck**, the **trucks**, and the wheels. The deck is the flat, top part of the board. Most decks are made of layers of maple wood.

The trucks connect the deck to the wheels. They are usually made of **aluminum**. Skateboard wheels vary in size, color, and hardness. They are made of a tough material called **polyurethane**. Skaters choose wheels based on their style of skateboarding.

Skaters also need safety gear. Elbow pads, knee pads, and helmets protect riders when they fall.

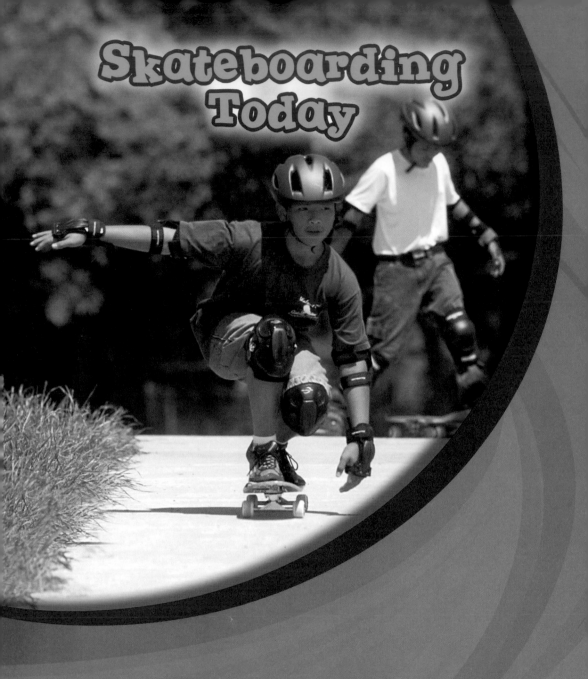

Skateboarding Today

Today, skateboarding is a worldwide sport. Many skateboarders like to cruise down streets or sidewalks.

Some take their boards to **skate parks** to try some tricks. The best skateboarders can become professionals.

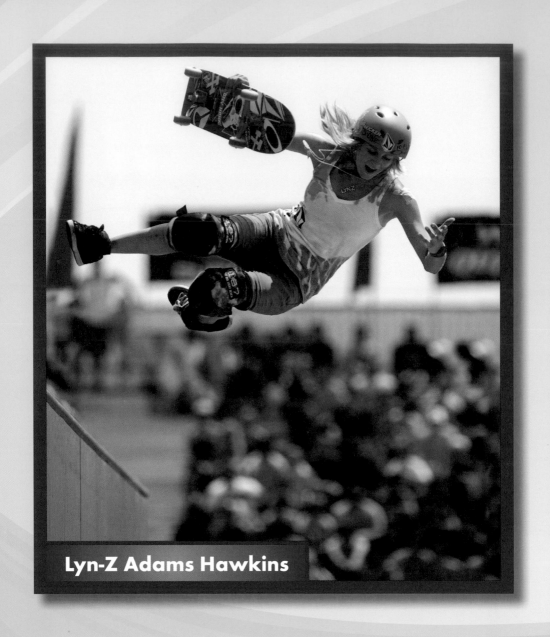

Lyn-Z Adams Hawkins

Fans love to see the best skateboarders go head-to-head. They go to Summer X Games and World Cup Skateboarding events to see the sport's top stars.

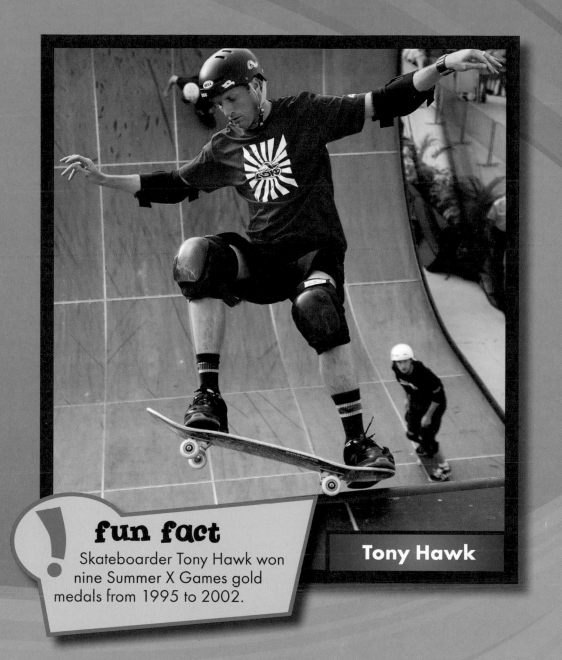

fun fact

Skateboarder Tony Hawk won nine Summer X Games gold medals from 1995 to 2002.

Tony Hawk

Skateboarders like Tony Hawk and Lyn-Z Adams Hawkins inspire skateboarders of all ages. Do you think you have what it takes to skateboard like a pro?

Glossary

aluminum—a strong, lightweight metal

deck—the flat, top part of a skateboard

grabs—tricks in which a skateboarder grabs part of the board while in the air

half-pipe—a type of ramp that is shaped like a "U"

polyurethane—a hard, durable plastic material used to make skateboard wheels

professionals—people who are paid to play a sport

ramps—sloped inclines that skateboarders jump off to do tricks

skate parks—paved areas built for skateboarders; skate parks usually include ramps, rails, and other obstacles.

slalom—a type of downhill race in which racers must weave between a series of gates

street—a type of skateboarding competition in which skaters do tricks on a series of obstacles on the ground

Summer X Games—a popular competition for a wide range of action sports, including skateboarding

trucks—the parts of a skateboard that connect the deck to the wheels

vert—a type of skateboarding competition in which skaters ride on tall vert ramps, which have a vertical, or straight up-and-down, angle at the top

To Learn More

AT THE LIBRARY

Fitzpatrick, Jim. *Tony Hawk*. Chanhassen, Minn.: Child's World, 2007.

Streissguth, Thomas. *Skateboard Vert*. Minneapolis, Minn.: Bellwether Media, 2008.

Streissguth, Thomas. *Skateboarding Street Style*. Minneapolis, Minn.: Bellwether Media, 2008.

ON THE WEB

Learning more about skateboarding is as easy as 1, 2, 3.

1. Go to www.factsurfer.com.

2. Enter "skateboarding" into the search box.

3. Click the "Surf" button and you will see a list of related Web sites.

With factsurfer.com, finding more information is just a click away.

Index